VICKI LANSKY

A

Fireside

Book

PUBLISHED BY SIMON & SCHUSTER

NEW YORK   LONDON   TORONTO

SIDNEY   TOKYO   SINGAPORE

1 0 1

WAYS

To Say

I LOVE

YOU

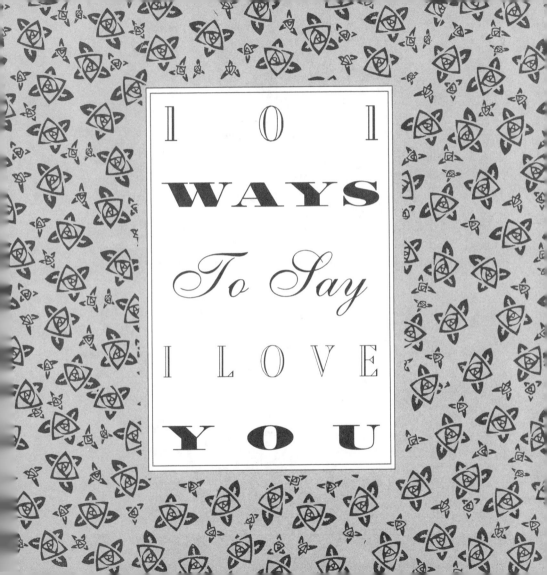

F

FIRESIDE
Simon & Schuster Building
Rockefeller Center
1230 Avenue of the Americas
New York, New York 10020

Copyright © 1991 by Vicki Lansky

FIRESIDE and colophon are registered
trademarks of Simon & Schuster

DESIGNED BY BONNI LEON

Manufactured in the United States of America

1 3 5 7 9 10 8 6 4 2

Library of Congress Cataloging in Publication Data
Lansky, Vicki.
101 ways to say "I love you" / Vicki Lansky.
p.   cm.
"A Fireside book."
1. Love—Miscellanea.   I. Title.   II. Title: One
hundred and one ways to say "I love you."
III. Title: One hundred one ways to say
"I love you."
HQ801.L295   1991

306.7—dc20   90-26838
                                                  CIP

ISBN 0-671-72350-2

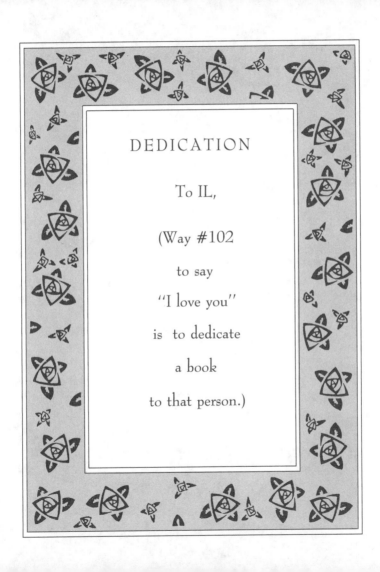

DEDICATION

To IL,

(Way #102

to say

"I love you"

is to dedicate

a book

to that person.)

$\mathscr{L}$ove Isn't Love Until You
∴ Give It Away
Being loved and valued as a
person is fundamental to everyone's personal growth and
development. It is the basis of
our own self-esteem, feelings
of self-confidence, and belief
in the security our world of-
fers us.

Feeling loved *does* make a
difference.

Some people have been brought up to feel they should hold back on loving words and actions. Others hold back because they've never *practiced* overt expressions of love, which now make them feel uncomfortable. Still others hold back out of forgetfulness. We're too busy, too preoccupied, or not around at the right time.

We may say "I love you" to the one we love but often, after time, the words become mechanical, as automatically given and received as "please" and "thank you." We may feel we express our love through our caretaking chores, financial support, and companionship. Oh yes, we may show it in an occasional surge of spontaneous affection, in shared laughter, in tender moments, in hugs and kisses. But it's the little things we do for each other that show our constant love. The actions. The surprises. Regardless of how we express it, love isn't love until we give it away.

Here are 101 ideas to trigger your imagination and help you think of many more wonderful ways to give your love away to the one who matters most in your life.

Vicki Lansky

1

$\mathscr{C}$reate a crossword puzzle using as clues "inside information" only the two of you know about.

$\mathscr{R}$ent a sentimental or
romantic movie
(and the VCR to play it on, if
necessary) for an enchanting
evening together. Make
buttered popcorn.

3

$\mathscr{P}$ut together a small photo
album or scrapbook of
the best of your times together.

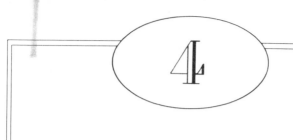

Tape your own readings of love sonnets or romantic passages. Or, if you have the voice for it, sing love songs.

$\mathscr{G}$ive a certificate for a

massage, facial, or

manicure. (Everyone, regardless

of sex or age, loves these!)

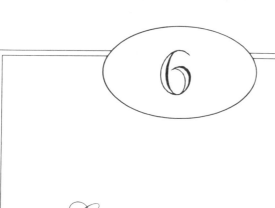

6

*C*all the radio station your
special one listens to and
dedicate a song to him or her.
(Be sure to catch the dedica-
tion on tape, in case it's missed.)

7

Write a history of your
romance in third-
person narrative and present it
on a special anniversary.

8

In a prominent spot leave a bowl of cherries with a note saying "Life with you is a bowl of cherries." Or leave a large jar of nuts with a note that says, "I'm nuts about you."

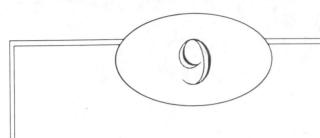

9

$\mathcal{S}$lip a new picture of you
into his or her wallet.

10

    $\mathscr{S}$end a surprise telegram declaring your undying love.

$\mathscr{S}$erve breakfast in bed.
— Even toast and coffee
becomes special.

12

*I*nterrupt your routine
and reschedule what's
usually a weekend treat—a play
or dinner out—for a
weekday night.

13

If your love has an
answering machine, call
and leave a mushy message.

14

$\mathscr{C}$all every hour one
afternoon with one
more reason you're glad
you're together.

15

*M*ail a week's worth of
anniversary or birthday
cards to arrive during the seven
days before the big event.

16

Declare your love in a
personals ad in the
newspaper.

Leave a love note under a
pillow, in the bathroom,
on a cereal box, in a briefcase,
between the bread slices of a
sandwich—anywhere out of the
ordinary.

18

Draw a hot, scented bath for your someone. Set candles around for light, put soft music on the stereo, and hang a 'Do Not Disturb' sign on the door.

19

*W*rite a love letter.
 · Talk about your
feelings. Mail it, marked
"Personal and Confidential."

20

$\mathscr{I}$f your love has a favorite
dessert that is the spe-
cialty of a local restaurant, give
a certificate for a late-night
treat (for two of course).

21

Write a love letter on the
back of a jigsaw puzzle
and give it to your significant
one in pieces.

$\mathscr{C}$ancel an appointment so
the two of you can have
an unexpected time together.
Be sure to do something special.

23

$\mathcal{T}$ell your special one about
five or six of his or her
personal habits and/or character
traits you admire most.

*R*ent a stretch limousine
stocked with champagne
and hors d'oeuvres to take you
to dinner when least expected
but most needed.

$\mathcal{G}$ive a "Love Book" with
your special one's name
on the cover. On the first page
write: "I love you because . . ."
Write in the book whenever
the urge strikes.

26

"*Send*" a postcard while
you're on vacation to-
gether (put it on a pillow),
saying "Having a wonderful time.
Glad you're here!"

27

$\mathscr{V}$isit a local art museum
alone, learn about the
works with romantic themes,
and bring your special someone
back for a personal tour.

28

Send your valentine card via Valentine, VA, for a special stamp and greeting. (Address and stamp the card, put it in a large stamped envelope along with a note explaining that you want the Valentine postmark, and send it to Postmaster of Valentine, VA 23887-9988.)

29

$\mathcal{M}$istletoe works all year long: hang it over the shower or over the kitchen sink, or carry some in your pocket for use anytime.

*G*o for a mystery ride to an unannounced destination. Keep your companion guessing until you arrive at a favorite ice cream place, beach, or restaurant.

31

$\mathscr{W}$rite a loving message on
an inflated balloon to
be found in an unexpected
place, perhaps in the pantry or
under the bedcovers. Filling a
whole closet with balloons is
even more memorable.

32

$\mathcal{M}$ake up your own
personal "I love you"
code that can be used from
across the room anywhere:
a wink, a pull on the ear, a
rub of the shoulder. Use it
often.

33

Lie outside on a blanket
together on a fine
summer night and watch for
shooting stars. Or go for a walk
in the moonlight, or in a new
winter snow or a warm summer
rain.

34

So you hate baseball or the theater. Buy a pair of tickets to your love's favorite event anyway, and escort him or her there.

35

Write a love poem, have it transcribed by a professional calligrapher, frame it nicely, and present it as a gift—for no special occasion.

36

Take a stroll down memory lane. Talk about or write down and share how you fell in love and what you find lovable about each other.

37

Engage in some out-of-
character spontaneous play
when you're together—
a snowball fight, a chase around
the room, or a funny face.
Making contests can help bring
out your playful sides.

38

Make or buy a giant
cookie that can be
inscribed, using a tube of icing,
with a message of endearment.

39

$\overset{\cdot}{}\,$ Paint "I love you" with a bar of soap on your sweetheart's car window (on the outside, in reverse writing) as a surprise morning drive-time message. It will come off with a few spritzes of water and the windshield wipers.

Send a message of affection in a helium balloon with instructions to pop the balloon for the message.

41

$\mathscr{C}$ ut out a poem, cartoon,
or funny saying that
expresses your feelings from a
magazine or newspaper. Mount
it on a piece of stiff paper
(maybe covering it with plastic
and attaching a magnet
to the back) and send it as a gift.

42

*I*f you belong to a group
that publishes a newsletter or bulletin your special one reads, place a message where he or she will be bound to see it.

43

$\mathscr{P}$ost a "lawn sign" of your
love and affection. You
can find one in a party store or
you can make your own.

$\mathcal{G}$et a map of your city and
put a "heart" (sticker or
design) over your location with
a note reading something like,
"Home is where the heart is"
or "Love awaits you at 3342
Treelined Lane."

45

$\mathscr{S}$end flowers or a note of affection to your love's mom or dad with thanks for creating such a wonderful person. Your love will be sure to hear about it.

46

*G*ive a gift of a treasury book of love poems, with an inscription "Just because . . ."

47

$\mathcal{D}$eliver something special in
a heart-shaped box, be it
jelly beans, chocolates, or jewelry.

48

$\mathcal{G}$ive a coupon for one hour of "anything you'd like me to do," based on an hour's notice. (P.S. If YOU get one, don't use it to get the lawn mowed.)

Create a card or note that
says, "What's Love Got
to Do with It?" Inside, write
"everything!"

50

$\mathcal{L}$eave a small bouquet of
flowers for your love
where he or she would least ex-
pect it—in the bathroom, in the
refrigerator, or even on a
workbench in the garage. Or
send some flowers to his or her
place of business or school.

51

$\mathscr{S}$end some of your love
notes unsigned or "from
a secret admirer." Consider
saying you didn't send them,
if asked.

52

Leave an anonymous note for your love to pick up a package at a certain address at a certain time. Prearrange it so when they give their name the package will be presented to him or her. (Roses from a florist, pipe tobacco from a tobacco shop, a gift certificate to use then and there.)

A nice act of love is getting your special person's paperwork in order without throwing anything out. Try rewriting or typing an address book into a nice new one with room left to add. (Put your name and number in red with a small heart by your name!)

*S*urprise your honey with a clean car (do it yourself or use a car wash). Leave a little note on the dashboard.

$\mathcal{M}$ake a bookmark (with a
heart shape at the top,
or just with heart stickers) and
the words "I love you." Put it
in the book your love is reading.

Create your own romantic tale. Start the story with a lusty beginning, then go back and forth, each of you taking turns embellishing the story.

57

Shampoo your loved one's hair.

58

$\mathscr{H}$ave a photo taken of you
and your special one
together and put it into a new,
attractive frame for display.

59

$\mathcal{S}$ign up for a surprise
trial lesson of something
new and potentially interesting
to you both—an art class, a
cooking class, or scuba
lessons, perhaps.

60

$\mathscr{P}$lant a tree (or shrub if
space is limited) in honor
of your special relationship.

61

For a warm wrap-up,
sneak the towels away
while your love is taking a bath
and warm them in the dryer
for a few minutes.

$\mathscr{C}$arve your initials, with his
or hers, into a scrap of
wood or a bar of soap.

63

$\mathcal{H}$ave firewood delivered,
then deliver yourself
and the refreshments.

64

$\mathscr{S}$et an atmosphere by
lighting a room with
as many inexpensive small
votive candles as you can
manage.

*S*erve anything from
a breakfast bagel to
an elaborate dessert with a
romantic decoration from a
specialty bakery or a party
supply store.

66

Give a houseplant with the
note, "Our love is sure
to grow."

67

$\mathscr{F}$ill a small heart-shaped
box with Red Hots or just
chocolate chips and deliver it.

Get baby pictures of the two of you and photocopy them together. Below the picture, write "Our love was meant to be."

$\mathscr{P}$lan a gentle "roast" for your special person. Seat everyone at a long table, with the middle spot reserved for the roastee. Each person should take a turn telling a funny story, anecdote, or memory about your special person.

70

*H*ire an actor from a service—anything from a pretend gorilla to a belly dancer—to deliver your message or poem at your love's place of business. (No one's been fired for receiving such a gift yet.)

71

$\mathscr{S}$end a single
$\overline{\cdot}$ envelope of bubble
bath in a heart-shaped
card.

72

Buy some of those little candy hearts that have words on them—"Kiss Me," "I'm Yours"—to give your love.

73

$\mathscr{S}$end a quote or note
— "signed" by a famous
person such as Phil Donahue
("Your opinion will always be
listened to"), Baryshnikov's
("My heart leaps with joy when
we're together"), Barbra Strei-
sand's ("Together we make per-
fect harmony"), or Kermit the
Frog ("Will you share my lily
pad?").

74

$\mathcal{G}$ive each other the "Love
Coupons" in the back
of the book—good for a
kiss, hug, or anything at all.

$\frac{75}{\cdot}$ Give your love a personal check for a million dollars (or some obviously uncashable amount) as a token of your affection.

76

$\mathcal{F}$ill up a heart-shaped box
with love slogans and
give it to your love. (Some
examples for the creator:
*Come Live with Me and Be My
Love, Love Makes the World
Go Round, Love Me Tender,
Love Is Like a Red Red Rose,
To Know You Is to Love You,
Love Conquers All, Love at First
Sight, Love Thine Enemy.*)

$\mathcal{M}$ake a chocolate mousse
in a heart-shaped mold.

78

Make a giant "Hershey Kiss" from the traditional Rice Krispies and marshmallow recipe. Wrap it in aluminum foil and add a paper tag on top with your special message.

79

*T*ell your love, after a
· sumptuous meal,
that all your refreshments
have been aphrodisiacs.

80

$\mathcal{F}$or women only: send
a kiss by mail. Put on
fresh lipstick and with lips just
open, blot on a note card. Send
with or without a message.

81

$\mathcal{W}$rite love notes using a $\dot{\overline{}}$ heart where the letter *O* goes.

82

$\mathcal{S}$ay "I'll clean up/do the
laundry/walk the dog, etc."
Then do it.

83

Stamp out a heart and
write "I Love You" in
the snow where your loved one
is sure to see it.

$\mathscr{H}$ave a meal delivered
$\overline{\cdot}$ . . . in bed, at
dinnertime, or as a
lunch surprise at work.

85

Pick a picturesque
bed-and-
breakfast inn
when going away
for a weekend
or a vacation.
They're romantic
and personal.

86

$\mathcal{P}$ick a bouquet of wildflowers
in the spring.

$\mathcal{L}$eave a surprise love message on his/her computer. (Enlist a coworker to enter the message on a computer at work.)

88

Acknowledge your loved
one's feelings, even if
you can't agree with him or her.

Surprise your love with a
glass of orange juice or a
cup of coffee or tea when he/
she steps out of the shower.

*A*dd a dimmer to your
bedroom light switch.

91

During the next summer rain shower (not an electrical storm), dress down and go for a walk together—*without* an umbrella.

92

$\mathcal{G}$o to a hotel for a night or a weekend in town and get the best room you can afford. (They often offer special weekend rates.)

*D*rop a chocolate kiss
candy in a jacket pocket
as a loving surprise.

94

Take ballroom-dancing lessons together.

When walking down a hallway or around a corner, pull your honey aside to deliver a spontaneous kiss.

96

$\mathscr{L}$eave your love a surprise note on the car visor.

97

"Warm up" your honey's
·   side of the bed while
waiting for him or her.

98

$\mathcal{S}$peak to your love daily
— during working hours,
even if only for a minute
(if your job allows).

99

$\mathscr{S}$cent any cards or
$\overline{\;\cdot\;}$ valentines you give or
send to your honey.

100

$\mathcal{M}$ark a date on his/her office or home calendar that's blank with a code word like "out." Then make your own "date."

101

Compliment your love
at least once a day about
something—anything.

A

TOKEN OF MY
LOVE

REDEEM FOR

A

TOKEN OF MY

LOVE

REDEEM FOR

A

TOKEN OF MY

LOVE

REDEEM FOR

A
TOKEN OF MY
LOVE

REDEEM FOR

A

TOKEN OF MY
LOVE

REDEEM FOR

A

TOKEN OF MY
L O V E

REDEEM FOR

A

TOKEN OF MY

LOVE

REDEEM FOR

$\mathcal{D}$o you have a favorite ÷ "I Love You" that we didn't include? Send yours to:

Vicki Lansky
% Practical Parenting
Department L-SS
Deephaven, MN 55391

For a free catalog of
Vicki Lansky's other
books, just drop a note
to:

Vicki Lansky
℅ Practical Parenting
Department L-SS
Deephaven, MN 55391

or call 1-800-255-3379
for a copy.